even a...
tread softly

a mothers' union anthology of poetry

even angels tread softly

Mothers' Union
Mary Sumner House
24 Tufton Street
London SW1P 3RB
020 7222 5533
email mu@themothersunion.org
www.themothersunion.org

ISBN 0 85943 064 2

Produced by MU enterprises Ltd
Printed by Gallpen, Norwich

contents

Foreword

I am delighted to celebrate with you this superb collection of poetry, written entirely by members, part of the 3 million we now have around the world. Poetry has long been one of my special joys and I know that I am going to use this book to soothe my spirit for many years to come.

These poems explore every facet of our life with a tender honesty and often with pain or humour. The breadth of style, emotion and experience leap off the pages with extraordinary power.

Our talented members express ideas as they emerge from the heart. And in catching any part of their essence, we receive a real gift where even angels tread softly... Read and enjoy...you will feel better for doing so.

Trish Heywood.

Trish Heywood
Mothers' Union World Wide President

genesis

in the beginning

In the beginning
God was the void,
for whatever is every-thing
must also be no-thing
and the void was water
which contained
all possibilities
and potentials
and the water played with itself
until she wanted more,
a desire for sunlight
to dance with
and play in
– or are you playing games with me,
just another trick of the light?
But it seemed to me
       (yesterday, watching the sun
       and the Thames playing
       and dancing,
       sparkle and shadow,
       depth and shallow
       and all the shades of grey) –
that that is how it could have been.

Liz Knowles

hear me

I am not yet born,
hear me.

For I fear the perilous creatures:
the sharks with menacing razors that plunge into flesh.
Crocodiles: crafty, a camouflaged predator.
The snake, king of all the reptiles: sly, slithering, baring its
venomous fangs.
The unmerciful eagles with tortuous, tearing talons.

Be thou near me.

I am not yet born,
protect me.

Protect me from the pain of an empty belly.
Shield me from the cold and icy winds.
Keep me free from attack and safe in the company of
true friends.

Oh save me!

I am not yet born.
Sense me.

Oh give me eyes to see the wonders of God's creation,
a nose to smell the fresh home-baked bread,
ears to hear the animals and birds of the earth.
A heart to love.

Oh help me!

Matthew Rodger

making the word flesh

Making the Word flesh
was woman's labour –
in the secret darkness
of the miracle womb
cells divide, grow,
shape and form,
in warm rich fluid,
cushioned, protected.

Each and every time,
by this strange and blessed timing
of our conjunctions,
we meet, and knit flesh
from ourselves to create.

However much we know
of our own biology,
there will still be that chasm
between the knowledge
– and the wonder of reality, newborn.

Liz Knowles

evolution?

If Man still walked upon all fours
we'd find it hard to open doors.
We'd have to buy two pairs of shoes
at twice the cost – gloves wouldn't do.
Ties and scarves would have to go
for fear of dragging in the snow.
Imagine all those proud new mums
with babies strapped beneath their tums.
The trade in backpacks would have soared;
at football, twice the chance to score.
Perhaps the best thought – sans our hands
computers could not invade our lands!

Margaret Fox

after darkness

... And then there was joy –
not a lot,
not even too well-defined,
but definitely ... a spark –
falling back into the dying embers,
re-igniting the flame
and bringing to birth
another spark.

... And then there was hope –
not much,
not in anything in particular,
but just ... hope –
like the tip of a young shoot peeping up
through the uniformly brown earth,
a small sign
of the life to follow.

... And then there was light –
not blazing sunshine,
not even yet the dawn of day,
but nevertheless ... one little shaft –
just enough to pierce the darkness
and show it for what it was;
just enough to remind me
that darkness submits to light,
that light finds its way
through the tiniest of cracks
into the darkest of places.

Catherine Aldis

Photo: Fleur Dorrell

how great thou art

And God said, "Let there be light."
Sun shone on snow at dawn in February.
Amidst the rain and despondency,
a rainbow yesterday shouted
"He is still there".

The night sky shows Orion's belt,
bright Venus and a dying space station.
We are busy interfering
in all that God has made.
O Lord forgive.

An Irish yew had to be cut down
before the Autumn gales blew it over
onto our gardens and homes.
The gulls are courting now
where a nightingale sang.

God sent His only son to us
to have no home nor rest.
But to take upon Himself
our guilt and grief.
O Lord forgive.

When the time comes for us
to join those who worship You
into eternity, help us all
to rest with You; now and
for evermore.

Ros McLachlan

quiet time

Dawn breaks through my troubled sleep
and, tossed about like the trees
outside my window.
By many dreams and anxious thoughts
your Presence descends and holds me.

As the cat curled on my lap,
I rest in the comfort of Your Love,
secure that all is in your Hand – Encompassed.

The wind blows from the sea
bringing rain to bless the earth;
and beyond the wind on some far shore,
twilight descends with the kiss
of the setting sun.

As the whole universe is held
in the hollow of Your Hand –
stars and planets
mountains and plains
forests and deserts
sunlight and rains,
so my life is a whole in You –
birth and childhood
marriage and family
joys and sorrows
health and infirmity.

You planned the whole but not till
Eternity
will I be complete.

Val Davies

the word of god

Brighter than a star,
Deeper than the sea,
Gentler than a dove,
Higher than heaven,
Quicker than light,
Sharper than flint,
Stronger than steel,
Sweeter than honey
Wider than the ocean,
That is the word of God to me!

Lagos Diocese, Nigeria

a day is born

Gone the shroud of darkness,
light filters through the air.
The rising sun
a crimson flare,
brings in on cue
the feathered choir.

Dew, a diamond carpet
covers all the land.
Unseen, the cuckoo
calls with mirth.
Bushes laced with cobwebs
night has given birth.

Joan Blake

naming

Before blackbird
was blackbird,
he was darkness
touched with gold.
He was the seed
of an unknown song,
a blueprint for flight.

Before hawthorn
was hawthorn,
she was perfume
on the breeze.
She was the sound
of strength,
the reaching forth of life.

Now, blackbird
in the hawthorn tree,
is a perfumed song
on a spring morning.
The merging
of two joys in
one uplifted heart.

Maureen G Coppack

the next eden

So many letters
need to be written
to redress the wrongs
being done.

But what is one voice
in this mad, man-made world
of cruel corruption;
the uncaring greed,
and wanton destruction
in the face
of Earth's need?

That voice
is the clarion call
and the beating drum,
protecting God's promise
of what is
to come.

So join with that voice
and do what you can
to help re-create
the next Eden
for man.

Zoe Woods

christ cycle

what is christmas?

Name listing, gift searching,
parcel packing, card sending,
pudding steaming, mince pie making,
turkey stuffing, stocking hanging,
party going?
Stars glistening, angels singing,
shepherds watching, stable sheltering,
Mary birthing, Joseph sighing,
lambs bleating, kings arriving,
Herod fearing?

Iris Lewis

have you time for me?

Hustling, bustling, buying, packing,
have you time for me?
Writing, signing, stamping, posting
have you time for me?
Making, rolling, steaming, baking,
have you time for me?
Icing, stuffing, decorating,
have you *time* for me?
Because of me you're celebrating,
lighting up the tree,
because of me there's carol singing,
crackers, fun and spree,
because of me the star was shining,
Wise men there were three,
because of me the sheep were bleating,
shepherds came to see,
I am Jesus Christ your Saviour
please make time for me.

Iris Lewis

miracle trip

When we landed
at Sinai,
who dared glance
into your eyes?

You were
huge
like angry bears,
powerful
as detonated explosives;
So different and transcendent.
How could Your will
be rich for me?

But when we met
at Bethlehem,
you landed
soft as dew
on a silken petal
in a manger.

Yes, you were
meek and mighty at Jordan,
valiant and majestic in that desert,
generous in Cana,
Lord over the realms of demons
King over the realms of the dead,
always Master
over matter!

And
on that dark Jerusalem noon
you dived into the cold venoms of hell.
You swam through the very stings of death
detoxifying being
as Easter morning breaks.

Now Welcome Back
from your Father's glorious throne,
we can hear
the precious, rushing sounds.
We can see
the glowing, cloven sparks
of your Spirit, Love and Power.

So
open Your Will
and show its absolute Good.
Open Your Word
and spread out pure Truth;
pour Your Spirit
and send down His sheer Delight.
Please take
this heart, soul and power
let them make
parts of Your glorious Throne.

Malomo – Kwara Diocese, Nigeria

the carpenter's son

Like any son, he'd watch and learn
the use of chisel, saw and plane:
he'd help his Dad, hand up the nails,
see hammer strike home true –
then learn to do the same himself
with cast-off nails and unused ends.

Later, apprenticed to the trade,
he'd learn the qualities of wood:
its grains and surfaces, its knots,
which timber suited best each task
and how to finish work begun.

Did he, the dear Lord, choose this home
that he might be a carpenter?
That wood and nails should earn his bread,
the very tools with which he'd buy
Redemption? Become, through agony of nails
our Bread of Life, complete his task,
cry "Consummatus est?"

Joyce Donoghue

crucifixus est

I bring you
my anger and my pain
and beneath your feet,
I nail them to the tree
with the splinters of my hope.

Forgive me for I have sinned,
love me, for I have nothing else.

Liz Knowles

once on a friday ...

Watch now the Master Carpenter
offer himself in sacrifice:
see unskilled hands, unfeeling, drive
their nails through living hands,
impale him on their rough-hewn planks,
then raise him up ... and watch him die.
Gracious, he prays:
"Father, forgive ...
they do not understand,"
speaks words of welcome to the thief
who in extremis knows him Lord;
entrusts his mother to his friend ...
and then, and only then,
his care for others now complete,
from depths of desolation, comes
the loneliest, saddest cry:
"My God" – not "Abba" now –
"Why, why has thou forsaken me?"
Another pause - Satan still whispering
"Why not indeed come down?
Who then could disbelieve?" –
Final temptation this: Gethsemane again;
Is there no other way?

He cries,
a great cry that the watchers do not understand –
and then, that battle won,
the voluntary sacrifice, the final act of love.
Enveloped in our sin, weighed down
in darkness, agonised, yet trusting still,
as last he sighs "Tis done!" and softly breathes
"Father, into your hands …"
The victory won, the Son of Man departs
and mortal men, disturbed,
survey what they have done.
The Crucified hangs limp upon his cross –
untenanted, his body waits
for gentle human hands;
His spirit gathers strength for Easter's Resurrection.

Joyce Donoghue

whit sunday, fontanelas

Whit Sunday came concealed,
mist wrapped, mysterious,
a soft and subtle drenching, almost white:
and standing there I saw
that what obscures – half the garden blotted out –
also reveals.
The mist
scrolled shapes before me and made visible the wind.

Susan Latimer

pentecost

Bereft. We clustered
like pups for communal warmth –
searching for our easy milk.
Like mothers' milk it came,
sudden, painful, for all – at once.

No slow, ripening growth for us.
Instant. Enabled now.
Our Good News. Deep within us
freed – for those with ears
and understanding of the cost.

No private pleasure or slow delight
no time to digest
no more barrier of language.
Forced to answer, because we can.
Called to account
for our performance.

Irene Greenman

pentecost

Come Holy Spirit
fill the spaces,
reign in the corners
take all the places,
drive out our sin,
deceit and the lies,
let good enter in.
Open our eyes
guide every mind,
put love in each heart.
Help us to find
where we should start
to live as your word
tells us to do,
seeking perfection, Lord,
and closer to you.

Geraldine Laker

the wind in the trees

trinity house

Beyond the sheep-short grass
ghosts of long-past life emboss the cliff
that swoops to the battering sea.
Sleek shags hang out their wings to air
and kittiwakes plane and swerve,
and the little bull-headed martin burrows and survives.

Stack and step
reef and stealthy sand
and the purposeless commotion of the waves,
innocently and incessantly menace the late-comer,
man:
determined to walk on water,
he has built himself the wherewithal to do it.

Then, to protect him, all around the coast,
close in to land or far,
lighthouses he makes; staddled deep in rock,
lightships fast-anchored in a known and constant place;
and their signs of light
seen and understood and turned into action,
will bring him safe to the land.

O Father, my steadfast rock, my fixed anchor,
Son, my steady light across the darkness,
Spirit, my watchman and navigator, my will to act aright,
at the end bring me, too, safe to the land.

Freda H Cave

muchelney – a villanelle

An ancient breathing stirs within those walls:
spirits? – the word too firmly shapes the air
where cowl and sandal moved along the halls;

from dorter roof a cool grey stockdove calls,
then briefly checks, as if he listens where
an ancient breathing stirs within those walls;

near quiet stones, where yellow lichen crawls,
thyme grows, and trefoil, and the little tare,
where cowl and sandal moved along the halls …

Then, when a vast night sky the mind appals,
remember how in Wessex wetlands fair
an ancient breathing stirs within those walls,

forgotten music still the ear enthrals
through silence more than man today can bear,
where cowl and sandal moved along the halls:

And winter evenings, when the cold light falls
to lonely silver gleam, recall how there
an ancient breathing stirs within those walls
where cowl and sandal moved along the halls.

Freda H Cave

holy island

Breath of the wind – soft and gentle,
little waves chuckling on the shore,
a flock of birds
clackering across the sky,
grasses ruffling in the breeze and dancing in the wind,
plants full of seeds – birds greedily flitting to and fro
the great wide sky and the little bit of earth beneath my feet.

Iris B Cox

open the curtains

Open the curtains,
let in the light.
Look for the dawn,
morning's beginning.
Gaze,
enjoy,
exult.

Open the curtains
let in your life.
Look for creation,
shoots of new growth.
Nurture,
encourage
to fruition.

Patricia Newland

pearl fisher

A man stands in man's element, the day,
shouldering the light and friendly air,
poised to pitch further than sight:

willingly is it he goes?
drops down through clear blue, to clouding green,
to an eye-foiling gloom
where shapes loom like alien midnight fears
that brush along the mind and slide away
unidentified …

but to go down, and go down, into fathomless night –
when nature urges up toward the sun,
and to stretch open
eyes not made for the sea's weight and sting –

to where, among the dregs of sea-years,
lies the precious jewel, stone-trapped, cold and still,
helpless and alone, unless a man should bring
the power in his mind and in his hand:

lungs cracking with lifeless breath
yet must help him rise and break the line
between two lives:
lungs clawing for new air
are agony of death
or of birth into another life:

with a shout
he holds aloft his prize
an offering to the all-fathering sun …

it is your Easter, Lord –
and mine.

Freda H Cave

tranquillity

Soft soothing notes of an orchestra
drift across her senses.
Words on the page imbued with hidden meaning,
strike chords within her heart
of remembered times, feelings –
tugging her heart strings
with memories of love.

Through the window are snowdrops –
pure white and virginal.
Bare branches of the lilac tree
reach to the grey sky above.
A gentle maiden stands, still and tranquil,
beside pots of pale green leaves
and the trellis fence.

Outside the January air is chill,
but inside is warmth and security.
Sleepy cat curled on her lap
purrs contentedly, sharing her mood
of peace and tranquillity.

Val Davies

the waterfall

A hidden place – steep, winding steps
lead you there, into the secret
and secluded glen.

From under the mossy stone wall
the dark waters emerge, flowing
into a deep pool.

Then to tumble, leaping, splashing
outrageously, joyously free
to the stream below …

Which glides and flows over rocks
under summer's bright green canopy
to the waiting meadows.

On another May evening
she first came here, sorrowing,
alone and searching,

And the secret waterfall, so
wonderful, so unexpected
caused the tears to flow.

Now returning, still needing love,
she watches the water, flowing
surely and happily …

Carelessly, 'neath its bright canopy,
refreshing and nourishing the
meadows in its path.

Could she, like the waterfall,
be filled with living water
and overflow with joy?

Val Davies

harmony

Every tiny ant or bee
Works in perfect harmony
Man, who claims superior wisdom,
Could learn a thing or two from them.

Margaret Fox

a place of peace

Arched, silent and empty,
yet full of grace –
this place –
not beautiful, but prayed in –
rests in my heart.

Patricia Newland

another spring

Even in winter the garden can be beautiful:
colours are subtle, restful after ripeness,
bare stems indicate where summer's flowers
flourished,
and here and there I see
      a small green pointer to the spring.

Even in winter a person can be beautiful:
love shines out of tired yet tender eyes;
a warmth belies the cool hands which hold their
comfort still.
In you a sense of life beneath,
      awaiting a different spring.

Dawn Bruin

lord of the dawn

Lord of the dawn, praise to Thee.
Praise for the streaks of light,
Praise for the hills lighted up,
Praise for the Solway shot with light,
Praise for the shore alive with birds,
Praise for the waders chorus,
Praise for the new day and new sky.
Lord praise for ears and eyes that work.

Jean Black

the mystery of autumn

I am a tall tree with my feet in the ground,
where I feel safe and basically sound,
the birds nestle in my leafy bowers,
O', how I love to shade the tiny flowers,
but when the days are turning cold and foggy,
I know my roots feel strangely boggy,
for this is the time for my leaves to change,
as if a new chapter has turned the page,
my precious leaves will soon be red and golden yellow,
giving a soft touch, that tends to mellow,
but later my leaves will fall to give new birth,
for this is my sacrifice to the earth,
to enrich the ground for seeds to grow,
at my tangled roots deep down below,
so this is my sacrifice I bring each season,
for our God has His special reason,
He gave us Jesus, a sacrifice to bring new life,
to all who believe in His love and peace, delight!

Sheila Pope

god's kingdom

Should you wander from the pathway,
from the tended well cut highway,
through the brambles wild and prickly
past the piles of rotting leaf mould,
you will hold your breath in wonder
at the beauty hiding therein
at the awe inspiring splendour
of God's Kingdom gently nurtured.

Dainty Robin Redbreast trilling
gently sifts damp earth for insects,
Jenny Wren flits hither, thither,
butterflies display their colours,
sloe worms slide and slither homeward,
slugs and snails and creepy crawlies
share the garden moist with dewdrops:
angels' jewels dropped from Heaven.

Pamela Horton

wondrous earth

Hold firm your beauty
O dear earth
or men may steal
your wealth away.
They walk this earth
with eyes closed tight,
seeing the darkness
of the night.
Thunder rumbles
from on high.
Hush wondrous earth –
do not sigh.
The rainbow calms
the storm away,
the birds once more
fly safely home.

Yvonne Moore

the bat

Orphan in the churchyard
tumbling from the tower,
sprawling, blind, bewildered;
completely in the power
of staring humans, wondering
at his tiny eerie face.
Caring, gently hiding him
in a shady, leafy place.

Trembling on the tree trunk
as noisily, boys play.
Cowering from the sunlight,
slumbering through the day.
Falling dusk, familiar sounds,
arousing, beckoning!
Fluttering forth on slender wings,
flying to family revelling.

Silhouettes in the sunset,
phantom shapes in flight,
darting, dancing, gliding,
squeaking with delight.
Munching moths and snapping gnats
'till midnight finds them clinging,
dreaming, hanging upside down
where morning bells were ringing.

Mrs F English

torn
tapestry

january

The very first day of the very first week
of the very first month of a brand new year,
so fresh and exciting, unused and unspoilt,
with the promise at last, of peace in my heart,
it's time to forget the hurt and the pain
to let go of the past and start living again.

Out in the garden, the cold winter wind
is tearing at trees and bending the grass,
whistling round corners, disturbing the dust,
finding cracks in the wall and escaping once more.
Cheerful and boisterous, it goes on its way
looking for mischief and more games to play.

Resolutions announced at the midnight hour
are rehearsed and repeated and promised again,
this year there'll be order, not chaos around
the home and the garden and all that I do.
I'll start as I mean to go on, this New Year,
looking forward with hope, I've nothing to fear.

The wind has grown weary, at last, of its games
giving way to the snow, which drifts slowly down
clothing pathways and grass and the dustbin lid
with a blanket as soft as a goose-down quilt.
Nurturing plants in the cold, bare earth
now awaiting the time of their own rebirth.

I open the box where my memories live,
sit on the floor and remember with thanks
the fun that we shared, the love and the warmth
and our plans for a future, that's now in the past.
I pray to the Lord that this day will be
the start of a year, that will change life for me.

Now the sun has come out, and because of the chill,
it's sparking off snowflakes and lighting the house
with a pale golden glow, which shows up the dust
in places forgotten, in the year that has passed.
Then the Lord gently closes the lid on pain,
and I know that today, I'll start living again.

Margaret Renner

my cocoon

This is my cocoon
inside it, metamorphose
into what?
Most creatures similarly designed
change into something more beautiful.
Who would prefer the caterpillar to the tortoiseshell?
Or the grey leatherjacket to the stately balletic cranefly?
My change is different,
I am becoming a skeletal apology of my former self.
The crab is eating me away,
the crab that is cancer.
My cocoon is sometimes invaded.
Trays come in bearing food I do not want
needles invade my body with fluids I need so much.
"Put you clean dear, make you look better."
Better! How can it be better?
I am in a cocoon; the world outside is not real.
I hear news of it, but it is apart from me.
"Do you want the wireless dear?"
"Listen to the news."
I am the news.
There is nothing else;
the faces that invade my cocoon bring something else,
they bring the only thing that matters.
They bring love
love, love, love
into my cocoon.
No butterfly has this,
he is not as lucky as I.

Patricia Layton (1940 - 1988)

sharing

I see your emptiness my friend,
alas – the broken heart I cannot mend.
I know your sorrow – yet cannot feel
it's depth of pain that is so real.

I try honestly to share
the loneliness which you must bear.
I am no use – this is your pain,
but time I know will heal again.

So what is left that I can do?
To ease the hurt and care for you.
Dare I so much to ask in prayer?
That you will soon be free of care.

To ask of Him, what I can't give,
the strength and courage just to live,
the hope for you to face each day,
that soon your grief will fade away.

Yes I can only share with you –
the knowledge of what God can do.
For each of us has different sorrows –
yet all of us need new tomorrows.

Judy Thomas

dad

So suddenly you went.
Glasses off, eyes rubbed.
A sigh and you had gone
beyond my grasp;
yet in that moment
you came to me;
busy at the sink,
miles apart, I felt your presence.
Your love surrounded me;
your last goodbye.

In that instant was gathered
all the years of love.
Conflict too;
so much of you in me.
Memories of childhood,
laughter, joy.
Advice not always heeded,
valued now.
Too late for thanks,
but love remains.

Beatrice Smith

anxiety's pay

Every time
I tried to climb
and spy out tomorrow

The stool would slip
and I would fall,
sliding into yesterday.

Today must have been slippery enough.
What was I peeping for?

Malomo – Kwara Diocese, Nigeria

healing

May this sorrow
be to you
an opening
for Christ
who, standing
in the gap,
will fill it
with his stature
will be himself
the interwoven patch
in the torn tapestry,
will himself work
your heart's hurt
into his own
maturity.

Penny Purry

why?

A beautiful spring afternoon,
traffic passing
on a busy road.
A car in the garage
ticking over,
sadness and death
to unfold.

Was your load too heavy
to carry?
Were you bullied?
Did you feel unwell?
Were you burdened?
No shoulder to lean on
no listening ear to tell.

You laboured and carried
without question.
Loyal to family and friend.
We never suspected
your torment,
or your life
suddenly to end.

The village is dark
since you left us.
To go where pain
and hurt cease.
We hope you found
that shoulder to lean on,
and everlasting peace.

Joan Blake

america
= 11th september 2001

Lord, we commend them to you
those who have gone before,
who suddenly and precipitously
arrive at Heaven's door.
Their last and only moment
too swift to say "goodbye"
and from those who loved them
the constant question "WHY?"
Why should evil triumph
as it seems to do today?
Lord have mercy on our world
and lead us on our way.

Our loving and our longing,
our struggles and our strife,
cease to have much meaning
when faced with loss of life.
So in all the anguish
the sorrow and the pain,
we commend them all to you Lord,
that your love will still remain.

Pat E Baly

september 11th 2001

This morning I donned my shroud,
– smart suit, high heels, handbag –
and strode out into my ordered commercial day.

Shortly after nine
– after coffee and doughnuts –
my shroud evaporated in incandescent colours,
red and orange, purple and blue.

I was pushed
– naked as the day I was born –
into a new day.

Cynthia Davies

alzheimer's

I AM here you know
trapped
inside this mind!

Behind these eyes lives a MAN
surprises YOU
doesn't it?

YOU think I don't know
feel
think
…exist!

I watch from inside my head
as he fondles you with
'come to bed' eyes.

"He doesn't understand"
you say,
letting him caress the sweet tips
which once swelled under my lips.

I lie in waiting,
trapped,
inside this mind
as you turn away
from my touch,
to dream of soft hands
with such Longing.

Your mango-scented hair
once soft and fair
now springy and grey,
cascades as you lay.
And you dream
a smile on your face
as you race
through memory lane
with him.

And I still lie
in waiting
trapped
inside this mind.

I watch you go to him
the one who used to be
ME.

Barbara Lightowler

fatman

Fujio's Mother is cooking a meal,
the table is ready and set,
but the family will never assemble again
for the meal that nobody ate.

Fatman belched, from his horrible breath
came a scorching, searing heat,
and his laughter roared as he ran down the road
hungry for human meat.

Fujio ran to the shelter.
"You can't catch me" he cried
but mother was trapped in the kitchen.
"The food is spoiled" she sighed.

Light the fire, pile the pyre,
let the flames burn warm and red.
Grandma says her rosary
for the children that are dead.

In the playground of terrible
memories, the games go on and on,
Fujio digs with a bamboo cane
for days that are lost and gone.

He sees Mother bent over the cooker
her face is blotchy and wet,
she cries for ever and ever
for the meal that nobody ate.

Penny Percy

a planned action

Few years back in this country, Nigeria,
night gave peace to every mind.
Returning home after the day's job,
the moonlight and stars were celebrated with wine
and telling of stories.

We played music loudly from our record players
as we expected, no gun-shots indeed.
Our doors and windows were then
good security guarantors.

But today it is a different story.
It calls for divine intervention.
To just sit and cry for help cannot give us good solution.
It is an emergency situation to everyone in this Nation.
Let us develop an alternative policy,
and carry out a Planned Action.

The government talks seriously about armed robbery.
Now who is to blame?
If we do nothing about it,
we will continue to be in perpetual fear.
Last night, neighbours broke down in tears.
It is an emergency case to everyone in this Nation.
Let us develop an alternative policy,
and carry out a Planned Action,
of fervent Prayers.

Mrs E O Ayadju

our dream

We had a dream of a family of our own,
a child skipping beside us, a small hand in ours,
the sound of laughter and the warmth of their love,
but our dream was slipping away.

In the beginning we shared our secret joy,
but it wasn't to be.
Four tiny angels touched us fleetingly and were gone,
their shadowy forms on a screen were all we ever
saw of them,
but the pictures remain etched in our memory for ever.

We'll never forget the many years of longing,
sadness like we'd never known and days of dark despair.
But you our children were the hope through those
dark days,
we held onto that tiny glimmer and then there came
a miracle.

Each time we'd ask if this would be the one,
could we ever dare to believe that you would stay.
We almost held our breath for those nine long months,
and then suddenly you were with us and part of our lives.

The time that used to go by so slowly began to fly by.
We saw tiny footprints emerging from a puddle on
the patio,
tiny handprints left on a window, and a smile that
melted our hearts.
We knew then that our prayers had been answered.

Then came a second miracle, something we'd only
ever dared to hope for.
Now there are two tiny toothbrushes next to ours,
two small pairs of wellies by the backdoor.
Happiness is ours and we know that we have been
truly blessed.

We used to have a dream of a family of our own.
Now there is someone skipping beside us, a small
hand holding ours.
There is the sound of laughter and the warmth of a
family's love.
We had a dream, our dream is here to stay.

Sandra Elliott

the canal of death

It was a calm Sunday evening,
no one suspected an unusual thing,
there was no indication that death was lurking,
around the hitherto serene setting.

As usual, people had left their homes,
some, to attend to religious worships,
others, to engage in social activities,
while children played in their vicinities.

Like a thunderbolt came repeated bomb explosions,
of monumental and unprecedented proportions,
and for dear lives, people ran in all directions,
but to no specific destinations.

Many fled to a Canal of water hyacinth for safety,
but sad enough got the antonym of safety,
as they were trapped and prevented from safety,
O my God! How elusive is this safety.

Who is to blame for this terrible thing?
What is the Authority doing to avert re-occurrence?
May the Almighty God prevent such a terrible thing
in this great nation from re-occurring.

Mrs H E Odeghe

earth
meets
heaven

the senses

I hear   a plane overhead, a car on the road.
The wind in the trees, rushing, swaying,
roaring, filling my senses;
it flows around me, blowing my hair,
filling my ears with its noise.

I see   so many things; details on gravestones,
flowers, their beauty, some faded;
the corn in the field; above my head
the church tower, seeming to move;
clouds scudding past and a watery sun
trying to shine;
all sorts of detail which I normally hurry past.

I breath in to **smell** – but there's nothing;
but in doing so my lungs are filled with fresh air.

I feel   beneath my feet the grass slippery on my shoes
and leaves beginning to turn, crunching as I walk.

No taste   but I remember the verse –
'O taste and see that the Lord is good'.
Amen

Angela Shipton

presence

Your solid bodies fill a little of the room,
two of you, lightly weaving words
on the loom of your time and space.

A blind-cord taps; the face of the younger
turns toward the window, smiling slightly:
Charlie again, she says – Charlie, the name
you use when inexplicable things happen –
a tap spurts, an untouched door clicks open:

It is not my name, but it is my self …

How, how to make you know that we are here?
Uncountable millions of us, in a little space
that three of you would crowd:
not the space that is full of you and your existence –
but this you have no image for, not yet …

There – the other of you looks up startled –
I coincided somehow with your senses,
made you aware – or was it something else? – of us here:

the presence and presentness of Eternity
crowding the vast emptiness of your air.

Freda H Cave

the walk

Give me a staff of roughly fashioned cane
that I may walk the path of life to You.
It will support me through the forest ways
and up the trail both treacherous and steep –
in verdant hollow and on stony paths,
on windswept plain and in the valley deep.
So, when I reach high moorland
where the air is thin
and stubby hillocks trap my weary feet
I'll pause, and leaning on my bough to rest,
reflect upon the trek which I have made –
before that last steep climb I'll make to meet
my Friend and Guide, who though it seemed
I was alone, unseen by me
has walked beside me as I make my journey home.

Brenda Cook

"we have seen the lord!"

I did not believe. I could not, without evidence,
perhaps because my pride prevented me.
Why should they see such things and I not there?
We gathered in the usual place, the upper room;
sat silent. Some stared at me expectantly.

Suddenly a rustling in the gloom,
a light, and there He was – or someone like.
"Peace to you all," He said, and then to me:
"Thomas, come here! Touch my wounds. You wished it."
I raised a trembling finger to His hand,
for a moment pressed it to the warm
moist place, and shuddered. Those strong fingers clenched.
I could not look at Him. "And now my side."

It was enough. "My Lord and God!" I cried.

Dawn Bruin

at the cross

earth meets heaven,
pain meets bliss,
sorrow meets joy,
sin meets grace,
fear meets faith,
law meets love,
absence meets presence,
death becomes life.

Patricia Newland

christianity

Who is my Lord?
Lightfoot by the lakeside,
leaving breath brief footprints in the grass
He is implied
rather than implicit;
a flicker in the corner of my eye, a shift of sun –
I can no more lay hands on him
than catch the wind.
But as the wind can touch and tremor me,
fan water out, stir sounds and scents,
so can he me.

Susan Latimer

Photo: George F. Mobley/National Geographic

the upper room

It was hot;
even now, with the sun set and the blue darkness
crept upon the house.
The rising moon cast shadows, violet shadows,
across the moonlight white stone steps;
old stone, warm still from the day's bright sun,
the stairway to the Upper Room.

"You go," the old woman said, "I'm hot and tired,
my knees are stiff and old. You go; you're young."
The girl, uncertain, paused;
should she attend upstairs, her mistress's domain?
Light, light at the top of the stairs, the door half open,
rushlight, moving shadows, hushed voices.

"Mind through," her mistress said, "tread carefully,
take care."
A flagon of wine stood ready, and Passover bread
wrapped in a white cloth, cool white linen.
The girl lifted the basket.
Her bare feet trod the warm stone, smooth and sandy,
feeling familiar dips worn by countless years of
climbing feet.

Was that a bird, a nightingale,
her sweet, soft song, clear in the scented air?
Straining to hear, the girl, mindless for a moment
of the load she carried,
there, on the last stone step, nearing the Upper Room
half turned, began to fall.

A shaft of light, the doorway stood wide open.
Strong hands restrained her, steadied her,
bore her load.
No voice admonished, scolded.
Gentle word comforted,
leaving her cry unuttered in her throat.
He smiled; but in his eyes were sorrow, love,
compassion and eternity.
And on the clean white cloth that wrapped the bread
a single drop of wine, like blood, was spilled.

Jacky Atkins

walking

Why did we do it?
there we were
minding our own business
mending the nets
hoping for a better catch tomorrow.

And there he was
Walking
Talking of fishing a different kind of fish
A crackpot
too long in the sun.

So, why am I here
and the others
following a man who is more than a man?
And why do I feel
with a lifting in my inner being
that I am not walking away

                    but

                        towards…

Anne Brown

the beloved

I saw him in the quiet
suburbs of my mind,
on the fringe of eternity
walking the halls of God.
A pure and living flame
touching with his presence
the blessed of his Father,
the light of the world
become the radiance of Heaven
and the new earth.
Where saints tread safely
surrounded by his abiding love.

Eunice M Carter

never alone

I come to meet with You in the silence,
and so quickly and quietly do You appear
that only I am aware You're near.
As I behold Your presence with me
time turns to gold and
I open myself up, to hold
all the love You would give.
You quieten the tumult of my heart
and it reposes in Your peace.
You calm my fears, and they become still,
you take my will and make it Yours.
You silence my whole mind
so that I am receptive
to Your thoughts, and You mould me
into a receptacle of Your love.
You empower me to pour its fragrance
upon Your sad and weary world.
As You kill the mean thought,
and quell the sharp retort, which would rise up
and exchange them for sweet words of love.
So You change me in our times together
where in the silence I surrender
and we merge and become as one.
You absorb me and I become part of You,
and when our times of silence are over
you accompany me wherever I go.
Enabling me to gaze at You in the still silent
centre of my heart, any time, anywhere,
allowing me to discover that because of my time
alone with You, I am never alone.

Margo Coser

what is love?

Love is a smile
and a welcoming voice
come in, sit down,
don't mind the noise,
the children are playing.

Love is listening
and caring
allowing the sharing
of anything that needs airing.
Not judging, but being there when needed.

Love is a hug,
and drinking a mug
of coffee with a friend
and time to spend
with them.

Love is seeing a need
then doing the deed.
Cooking a dish.
not saying I wish
I could help.

Love is the practical things.
Calling and caring
doing and sharing
all of which springs
from the Lord.

Jeannie Gye

now you are one

Marriage, a twining of two lives.
Yet twisted strands can fall apart
when tossed in the tempest of life.
A true braid needs three strands
interlacing it together
tightly, firmly
securely moored.
Entrust the Holy Spirit
to be your third strand.
He'll weave His holy essence
lovingly, invisibly,
protecting you from harm.
And all the love you feel today
will not dissipate
but expand and flourish,
binding you together,
tightly, passionately,
for all eternity.

Beryl Anderson

castleton

You went away,
but left me a dream land
to inherit:
beauty of sky and hill,
swift water
and sheep, high up on moors
where lapwings call.

It cannot match
the radiance of your City,
but surely
this high land, tranquil and clear
and kind,
must live in its shadow.

Carol Evans

playing the game

We sit cross-legged,
hands upturned like bowls
on the mountains of our knees.
Slowly, with eyes closed,
we count our breaths.
One ... two ... three ...

Except that I am cheating.
I am watching this streak of lightning
who is now
so unusually still and quiet.
Still, for the moments it takes
to count to twelve,
the highest number she knows.

Quiet, for the moments it takes
to make that first exploration of being
... of breath
...... of playing the game.

Maureen G Coppack

advanced feeling

I think
it will be a day
of naked terror
or
reposed in peace
of tremendous numen.

When
You are seated resplendent in glory
and
with Your majestic sceptre
of righteousness,
effortlessly
You stir the pot
of universal reality.

Ah!
When the swirl and the splash
have subsided
and true grains rise.

The boastful chaffs
will be swerving and swaying
waiting to be decanted
into final dust and fire.

Lord
my Lord,
that time
let all of mine
be found merry and gay
midst you fine
living grains.

Malomo – Kwara Diocese, Nigeria

dewdrops

Sunrise sparkling on the dewdrops.
A new day dawns
and God beckons us
beckons us, his people, from our slumbers
to awake.

As the smiling dewdrops sparkle
spreading God's sunshine
in rainbow hues
to be caught – and cherished – and loved
filling our hearts with joy and hope,
so let our own smiling faces
spread God's love
to each and every soul to pass our way
on this and every day
He gives us ...

Sunrise sparkling on the dewdrops
a new day dawns ...

Gwyn Harvey

colours of life

God gave us rainbows for our eyes to gaze upon and imagination to "see" the colours of life when darkness falls …

Yellow is the colour of Spring, the smell of daffodils, the warming rays of the sun on my face, the sound of bees and a spoonful of honey.

Orange is a summer's day, hot sand under my feet, ice-cream melting, warm bodies soaking up the sun, the heady smell of citrus flowers and the juicy tang of fruit.

Red is the heat of fire, the sound of traffic, a warning of danger, a blaze of anger, the smell of lipstick and the colour of passion.

Green is the smell of new-mown grass, the deepness of oceans, slippery moss on paths and springtime in the woods.

Brown is autumn leaves crackling underfoot, wood-smoke in the air, the taste of fresh gingerbread, the touch of animal hair and the closeness of friendship.

Blue is the colour of melancholy, the cold of winter, icicles hanging on a gate, a sign of regret and forget-me-nots.

Pink is a baby's breath on my cheek,
the softness of a lover's lips, velvet petals of a
full-blown rose and the first flush of love.

White is frost in the air, snowflakes on my face,
the innocence of first love, the pureness of a lily
and a young bride's wedding dress.

Black is the heaviness of sorrow, an ache of
loneliness, the smell of fear, and the home of
a myriad of stars in a night sky.

Purple is the badge of royalty and religion,
of death and mourning, and the smell of
fresh violets.

Grey is the colour of despair, a silent scream of
a soul in torment, the wings of a whispered
prayer and the softness of thistledown.

Silver is the clash of steel, tinkle of children's
laughter, the bubbling of a waterfall, the sparkle
in champagne, and birdsong at dawn.

Gold is the precious circle of love on a finger,
the promise of happiness and the love of God.

Margaret Renner

the breeze of love

I'm looking for the breeze of love.
I'm standing in the draught
of the window I've left open,
glancing fore and aft.
I'm hoping God is sending
someone to care for me,
and as I shiver in the breeze
I keep on looking to see.

Faith in God is essential.
Love? Is it there for me?
Hope? It springs eternal,
But there is no guarantee.

S F R Roome

i turn to
you

mary of bethany

I love Him so much!
He took me seriously, that day I was listening.
He brought back dear teasing, protecting, kind brother Lazarus.
I want to give Him something, while I have the chance.

But what is suitable?
He's always on the move, so nothing burdensome.
Whatever He freely receives, next moment He freely gives.
I want to give Him something, really and truly for Him.

In days to come
They'll pass round the collection plate at the offertory,
They'll sign on purchased bricks, or arrange for banker's orders.
I want to give Him something, a value beyond hard cash.

So here's my gift –
Cool alabaster from Egypt, the finest quality.
A pound of spikenard, nearly a whole year's wages worth.
I want to give Him something, a great unexpected surprise.

Can I pour on His head?
It might affect the food, or clash with the flavouring.
That kind of blessing should go only from greater to lesser.
I want to give Him something, glorious yet humble.

See, here are His feet.
I pull off the stopper, let the oil ooze out steadily.
Then break the jar open, scoop out the ointment residue.
I want to give Him something, these fragrant handfuls of love.

Senses run riot –
Old leper Simon's house breathes like a perfume distillery.
Spikenard drips on the floor, more than His skin can absorb.
I wanted to give Him something, but have I overdone it?

There's danger of slipping,
The Guest of Honour becoming a broken leg casualty!
Quick fingers dishevel the hair, and the loose knot tumbles.
I wanted to give Him something, but now I'm a fool.

Swab, wipe and mop.
Hair isn't made for this, but it's all that's available.
Compounding misery, there's talk about costly waste.
I wanted to give Him something, and I've made a hash of it.

"No, let her be."
His words are a balm to my soul, as soothing as ointment.
He knows my muddling love, sees further than I do.
I wanted to give Him something. My gift is accepted.

Mary Paterson

perspective

Take your troubles to the sea
and write them in the sand.
The tide will come and smooth them out
as if at God's command.
Walk back up to the cliff-top,
look down and you will learn
how small your problem really is.
The tide will always turn.

Sonia Forster

the prodigal

I have never aimed for perfection
not that
no, never that.
While you were busy being prodigal
I was wondering if I really could
turn the other cheek.
An eye for an eye dies hard
I find.
You seemed to be the one with everything going for you
yet now I find it was me all along.
Everything I ever do is wrong
in someone's eyes, somewhere,
nobody's perfect
certainly not me.

Though I was there all the time
I am the one
who needs to come home.

Liz Knowles

the penitent

She lies now where she fell,
thrown by hard hands
of harder men.
Her hair falling around her shoulders
gives scant protection from the cruel stones
that soon may shower upon her.
She bites her lip, lest she cry out in pain
as her accusers gather for the kill.
Oh, how she hates them – how she hates
all men, but chiefly these,
despising them for all the furtive ways
in which, at other times, they sought her out.
The Roman soldiers though, came openly
being so far away from home and kin.
Their crude jokes gave her no offence
her wit being a match for their obscenities.
These men had set a trap, and she,
poor wretched fool,
had failed to see their guile
and now was caught.

Who is this other man who, bending low
writes with a finger in the dust?
His voice rings out, 'Let him who has no sin
throw the first stone.'

Silence. Then comes the pad of sandalled feet
as one by one they leave the Temple Court.
He speaks again. 'Does no-one then condemn you?'
'No-one, my Lord.' Raising her head
she looks at him, but cannot meet
the gaze of those clear eyes.
He seems to see, not as did other men
her body, but her very soul wretched and guilt-stained.
'And nor do I pass judgment.'
'Go,' He says, 'and do not sin again.'
He takes her hand to raise her, and he smiles
though there is sadness in his eyes.
This man she does not hate –
here is a man whom she could truly love.
Her ordeal over, she may go in peace.

A penitent like her, I kneel beside a man;
his hand in blessing over me is raised.
He speaks. 'The Lord has put away your sins;
in peace then go.' And I, like her,
light-hearted go my way.

Rose Mackenzie

you call me to yourself

You call me to Yourself;
you draw me into Your presence,
to where even angels tread softly
and await Your word
with bated breath;
so I run to You, Lord,
believing in Your love,
relying on Your grace,
trusting in Jesus' blood –
and I find that You
have come to meet me
with arms open wide,
and have embraced me
before I am even halfway there.

Catherine Aldis

breath of god

In the same way that an eagle "stirs up her nest"
(Deut 32.11). So God pushes us out of our comfort zones.
He does this to encourage us to greater faith and
spiritual maturity.

Nudged out of the nest.
We plummet, paralysed with fear.

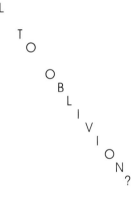

```
F
  R
    E
      E
        F
          A
            L
              L

              T
                O

                  O
                    B
                      L
                        I
                          V
                            I
                              O
                                N
                                  ?
```

NO!

God's promise wings beneath us.
"I WILL NEVER FAIL YOU."
No longer flapping feverishly, we learn to use adversity
as thermals,
to glide and soar above the world's constraints, and share
the Breath of God.

Mrs M Joyce Pitman

your love is great

Now that the well has gone dry,
and the clouds faded away,
the thick clouds of hope gone,
we stand, mocked by the wind
as it sways that tree before us,
laughing at our depressed situation.
But you are there speaking
in a thin, small voice
as you did to Elijah.
You have done it again.
When the firmaments and human beings
refuse giving the Comforting hand,
you showered your love
thus proving that "Your loving kindness"
is greater than life.

Victoria Nwaudo

"abide in me"

O Loving Father by whose hand
that pruner's knife is held
I shrink from what you need to do,
I fear this branch being felled.

Though not, O Lord, with one fell swoop
but much more gently done
with patience, love, and utmost skill,
until my will, with yours, is one.

And yet, dear Lord, I cannot say
to cut me with your skill,
for I flinch with fear of what it costs
to give you all ...yet still.

I long that this poor branch
may have its life renewed,
be truly with the Vine entwined,
with His own life imbued.

You heard that pleading prayer, then, Lord,
for life restored, for sap to flow,
for fruit upon the bough to form?
O love that will not let me go!
So as you live in me, my Lord,
transform this untrimmed vine,
renew the rotten, broken branch,
slowly change it into wine.

"Abide in Me and I in you"
so I need never fear.
If He is with me, come what may,
nothing is too great to bear.

Cherry Winder

god is my compass

Tho' the wind howls round about me,
I shall not be afraid,
as He cradles me e'er securely
in the hollow of His hand.
Nestled beneath the feathers
of His protection;
surrounded by His Peace, Stillness and Calm.

His banner over me is Love,
channelling the wind like a huge white sail;
the gentle Holy Spirit guides me on,
in the ebb and flow of the tides of life;
transforming even the fearsome breakers,
into beautiful ripples for my good.

His mighty tower of refuge,
like a lighthouse 'gainst the storms;
built with foundations deep
in the Rock of my Salvation.
You promised to be with me
when I pass through the waters,
I will be still and I will know
that You are near Lord;
and that You will teach me the way to go.

Margy

i will be your guide

Peace and love will follow me
and I will be your guide.
The deaf will hear, the blind will see,
peace and love will follow me.
When you are troubled, walk with me,
I'll be by your side.
Peace and love will follow me
and I will be your guide.

Elizabeth Graydon

precious saviour

You are my hope my consolation
in the gentle warmth of your love,
there is a strength that never fails,
a fortress and a hiding place
Where I need never fear.
Hold me close to your heart Faithful Shepherd,
shelter me in the haven of your presence,
help me rest in you and be at peace.

B J Hoff

dead in the night

Dead in the night, no moon, no stars.
The owl's hoot frightens both the living and the dead.
My only son falls and convulses,
the Devil is at it again.
Neither the monkey's skull nor the black oil
could ward off the devil.
Fear and trembling have taken over me.
The Lord won't allow this to happen
for He is my refuge and strength.
I call Him in the dead of the night
when neighbours are dead asleep.
Evil and agents of darkness prevail
in your great love, O Lord
you heard my cry for help
because you are always there
to answer my call.

Victoria Nwaudo

what is woman?

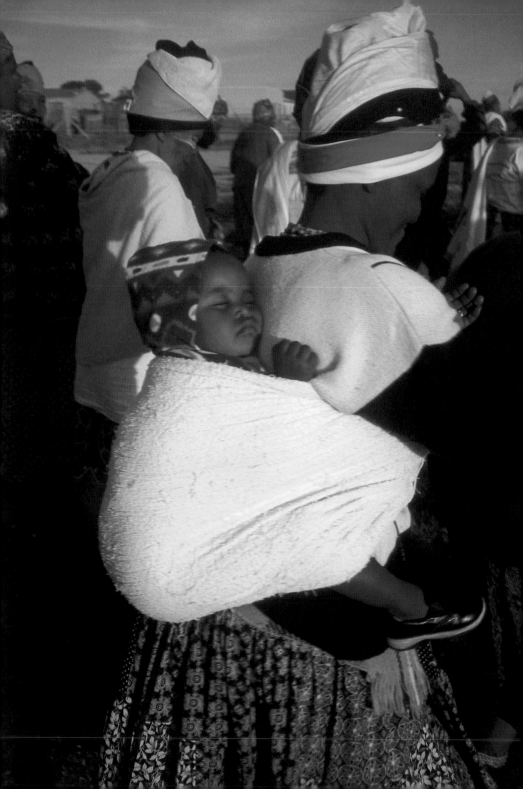

a prayer of an african woman

"I am a woman created in the image of God with dignity
and virtues, formed by the very hands of God,
given life by God's breath.

I am a woman, mother of kings and subordinates,
mother of ministers and housewives.

I am a woman, farmer, cook, housewife and neighbour
I work from morning till late at night, sow and reap
under the burning sun, go off with heavy burdens
and return home to feed my family.

I am a woman, a heart of my family. I am loved
and yet oppressed, held in esteem and still considered
inferior, caressed and yet beaten, indispensable
and still overlooked.

I am a woman. Lord you created me and
you know me. You know me by name, you
listen to me, when the world refuses to understand me.

You know all my worries, you see my tears
and hear my sighs, you are everything to me.
With you, Lord, there is hope.
In you I want always to put my trust as a woman."

Laura Katwesigye

uganda our home land!

Oh Uganda
my homeland
where the sun shines
all year round.
I delight in you
my motherland,
you feed me, educate me
and protect me
during times of turmoil.

Oh Uganda
you have survived
many decades of
economic disability,
political instability,
social incapability,
physical immobility,
and spiritual incompatibility.

Oh Uganda
the pearl of Africa you're called,
with beautiful mountains.
In the valleys, woman cultivates her crops
to feed the family and nation at large.
Disastrous it has been,
with torrential rains washing away
most crops and homes.
God bless our motherland!

Oh Uganda
You have elevated the woman.
Woman, mother of all humans
who used to till the land all her life
for economic sustenance
and physical survival.
Without her, life would be a failure.
God bless the woman --
Mother of all humans.

Laura Katwesigye

precious mother

Mother, you are so precious
you kick the dust each day,
on the bid to feed your children.
The heat of the Sun burns,
yet you forge ahead;
keep looking unto Christ,
who provides all your needs.

Precious mother, of the black,
your blackness could not hide
the whiteness of your teeth,
emitting rays of love.
The sweat from your toil could not
prevent your child's sleep, on your back
wrapped as Christ was
with a peaceful sleep in a manger.

Loving mother who goes hungry
as your children eat,
you became poor for them;
you sold your jewellery
for them to acquire white man's knowledge.
You emptied your whole self
as Christ did for the world,
which His love continually shows.
Do not mind the hardness of time,
your reward is great in heaven.

Victoria Nwaudo

a stressed woman from the rural areas (village)

Look at a woman
tired, hungry and stressed.
Baby clinging to her back
and she herself so tired,
she drags her legs.
The firewood, bundled on her head
weighs heavily
but still she trudges on.

Her skin, once smooth and lovely
is now muddled and dark.
Her clothes are dusty and torn,
her feet dirty and cracked.

The child cries. Stressed and
with parched throat but gentle voice,
she sings a soothing song,
she refuses pity.
Her arching, burdened back,
is a back that has submitted to
the hoe for hours on end.

Neither old, nor ugly
she is gentle, tireless and brave.
When she reaches home
she fetches water from the well,
lights the fire, prepares the food.
There's no more work in the fields
till the sunsets.
Dear God! When will she be stress free and rest?

Joyce Kinyua

oh women of uganda

Oh Women of Uganda!, what shall I call you?
I am desirous of giving you a name
but which one? Please advise me.
Which name should I give you?

Shall I call you tractors?
For you till the land you do not own.
Yes, you till the land all day long.
But what is your pay?
What does a tractor receive for tilling the land?
Please, help me to answer.

Oh Women of Uganda,
What shall I call you? I am desirous of giving you a name.
Women of Uganda, you deserve another name.
But which one? Please advise me.
Which name shall I give you?

Shall I call you factories? For you produce children
whom you neither own nor control.
Yes, you are factories
for you have no control over your uteruses.
You are better factories if you produce sons
but rejected factories if you produce girls.
But what is your pay?
What does a factory receive for production?
Please help me to answer.

Shall I call you donkeys?
Yes, you are donkeys.
For you are heavy laden
both on the head and at the back.
Today, a pot of water on the head, a baby at the back.
Tomorrow, a load of firewood and a seventh month pregnancy.

But what is your pay?
What does a donkey receive for carrying loads?
Please, help me to answer.

But Women of Uganda,
donkeys and tractors are treasured by
their owners and users,
and factories are great assets
but what about you?
Who knows your worth?
Beasts of burden they call you,
cattle is your name,
for they buy you with a bride price.

Women of Uganda, I mourn for you.
You are the centre of production
but at the periphery of benefit,
you hold half the sky on your head
and mankind in your hands
but you own nothing.
You have no home,
you only have one at the will of men,
you have no children.

Women of Uganda
for how long will you be silent?
Time has come that you must talk.
Yes, you must shout, so the world may hear
and society may understand.
And your cry for your rights may be granted
and Ah! A better name you shall get.

Betty Rukashazya

late start

Mature ladies, wanted to swim,
rushed to the pool, slow to get in.
Terrified,
clung to the rails,
instructor panicked,
thought they were whales.

Week by week, they volunteered.
Teased, mocked and jeered.
Chlorine in eyes,
stomach and throat,
six months later
able to float.

Fear of water, a thing of the past.
Butterfly swimmers, flying at last.
No longer feeling
old flabby fools,
instead, life-savers
at swimming pools.

Joan Blake

love

The painless point of cupid's dart,
the brand of a man in love, a mark.
The wound heals and grows a fairer skin,
and a newer life has entered in.
Now he has a purpose to fulfil,
to possess the woman of his heart, until
they find together the harmony in time
which time can never break, and stays immune,
from troubles of the changing world and heart,
always happy, joyful, never far apart.

Maurice Darbey

thank you god

Let's praise you God, our creator
for your love for the human being
when you gave him a suitable aid,
she received a good name, Mother of all those alive.
Thank you God.

The secret of prayer was revealed to one of this Mother's children.
She saw your light and founded the Mothers' Union
in England in 1876.
The one I praise for her bravery is Mary Sumner.
God really loved her.

As you so loved this Mother,
You let her family spread far and wide, worldwide,
wherever the Anglican Church was at home.
Later, in 1965, the MU was founded in Rwanda and
welcomed through open doors.
The mothers praised you and made branches in all the parishes.
And still today, we have brave women who carry on from 1965.
God you loved us.

Some among our elders at Kigeme continue to teach about
the Mothers' Union and enrol more mothers.
In 1992 you gave us our Kigeme Diocese and we knew God –
You loved us.

And now your love keeps coming!
We have a worker with a salary
and a car that climbs a thousand hills.
We praise you God.

And as you've blessed the work done here,
the family has grown – 34 branches with 829 enrolled members.
We will proclaim your good work everywhere.
God you will enable us and we praise you.

Let your organisation bear branches.
You haven't forsaken it.
You gave it brave mothers – Mvunabandi Virginie, the Head,
she works day and night to speed our progress on its way.
God help her.

The members meet regularly;
they pray, encourage one another and farm the land.
Even though the soil is acid, they toil away
and reap a good harvest of vegetables and crops.
You are all God.

God you gave us many gifts
so that we may use them for your glory:
animals to breed and share among our branches
knitting, sewing, embroidery, cooking.
God you loved us.

Love is the greatest gift.
It gathers us together;
we share our tasks, we talk of our
families, the education of our children.
We bring that love to people in need,
the poor, the lonely, widows and the sick.
God enable us.

As our aim is:
"I can do all things in Him who strengthens me"
we call upon you so that we can fight against poverty,
be more united and spread the good news of –
the Mothers' Union.
Thank you God.

Members of Kigeme Diocese, Rwanda

underground orphans

Huge-eyed emptiness of six year old's stare,
shrugging off her short life-time's undeserved cares;
shakes empty Ribena carton at me,
two coins clanking in remorseless despondency:
"Any change, Lady?
Any change to spare?"

Suckling baby sister bare-toed 'neath Mother's shawl,
young brother on blanket beginning to bawl.
Racket of Heathrow Shuttle thund'ring past,
waifs chilled to the marrow from stairwell's icy blast:
"Any change, Lady?
Any change to spare?"

Rounding the corner of the stair,
commuters glazed glances. Why should they care?
The cheek! Temerity to beg!
Sally Army keep an eye, takes soup, knows Mother as Meg.
"Any change, Lady?
Any change to spare?"

Pamela Horton

through the ages

youth

Our children's children
Take the stage
Which once we trod
With even gait.
Sure of tomorrow –
Now they rush
From one scene
To the next
Scattering time around them
Sure of their fate
Embracing life with all their might
Unafraid and full of song –
We stand by
And applaud their courage
Wishing them well
On life's great journey –
We hold them in our hearts
For ever more.

Jean Chartres

the days are passing my son

The days are passing when you will hit your drum to my beat.
Now you enjoy making your own rhythm.
When I listen carefully, I realise our one pulse beat has
become two.

There are fewer days when we harmonise our song,
now you prefer to make your own music.
Your song is yours and mine is mine, you say.

There are few days left when your gaze will centre on me
Now you look slightly to the side as I speak,
you squint to see further than close by.

The time is passing when you paint your picture to please me.
You now choose your own colours,
your own bold shades.
You no longer hold your breath and glance up to check for
my approval.

Your look of defiance gives me joy and sorrow in equal
measure –
joy is seeing you prepare for the flight from our nest,
sorrow because one day you will fly, albeit falteringly,
and soar on your own home-made wings.

The unclasping of your clenched nervous hands from mine
to push you
towards your first lonely experiences
will be reversed.
Instead *my* fingers will be trying to hold on to yours
perhaps even tighter, as, you,
without hesitation, unclasp my fingers from yours, and let go.

Matthew Griffiths

coloured milestones

White organdie dresses
and fluffy angora bonnets,
black patent shoes, bought for Whitsunday.
Long pink satin frock for walking with the Scholars
Uniforms, first brown then green and cream.

First grown-up coat, wine red
with nipped in waist and full skirt
very New Look!
Violet wool frock, worn at a dance
where I met my future husband.
Then white wedding gown
and pearly grey dress and coat
for going away.

A lemon and white carrycot
for bringing home our first daughter.
Used again for her sister who had a blue blanket
that I still cherish.
Halcyon childhood days,
multicoloured teenagers and
psychedelic music coming from both bedrooms
at the same time.

Then all too soon
white weddings, with touches of peach and yellow
young wives and busy mothers
each with their own coloured threads
to weave.

Now, more time to watch
iridescent pink sunrises,
white mist rolling along the valley
to the green hills above.
Fiery orange and gold sunsets
and indigo skies.

Grandmotherly grey, but with
a singing rainbow
in my heart
Praise the Lord.

Barbara Beard

eve and gordon

The drone of engines across the night sky
reminds me of you, and what might have been.
We were to be married
but you, dear Gordon, were sent abroad,
abroad to Africa, to Malta, Sicily, Italy,
pressing ever northward in the liberation of Europe.
Four long years have passed since you went away,
with only our letters to keep us in touch,
now the letters have stopped,
stopped by the letter that everyone dreads –
"Missing, believed killed."
Shot down; too low to bail out;
a ball of fire; no one could survive.

The thought of you gave me the will to live.
When the doctor dressed my burns
I thought of you at work –
your caring hands, your gentle voice
comforting the sick and wounded back home.
I thought of you during the weeks of captivity,
those weeks of forced marching
and of near starvation.
I thought of you with joy
when the prison camp was liberated.
At last the war is over and I am truly free,
free to come home to the land I love,
and to you, dear Eve, the girl I love.

Through all the years apart
we had dreamed of this day,
dreamed of running into each others arms,
now it is no dream. It is reality
but there are guards watching us
and we are both in uniform –
We salute!
We plan to marry straight away. What a rush.
A licence to get; the wedding dress out of wraps;
the reception; the honeymoon – but wait!
Are we the same people as when we parted?
Has the war changed us?
Will our love last?

Yes, through all the years since, our love has lasted.

Julia Hatfield

90 years

As dawn awakes and I must go
down to the Home – the one I loathe.
Dear God, why me?
I loved them all, each one from small;
the years have gone and with them youth.
Lonely thoughts and empty hours
Stretch out the day without the power
to do those things I once did do…
which leaves me now so sad and blue.
I ask you please my life to fill
I try so hard, but still …
The time has come when I must go
down to the Home – the one I loathe.
The babes I loved are now all grown
they need me not for I am old.
They say, "no burden you are Mum", but
the time has come when I must go
down to the Home – the one I loathe.
90 years I've served you Lord
I'm weary now and ask you please,
the years ahead to live with ease
in this Home you've planned for me.
I know, dear God, you're by my side
and knowing this, I will survive.

Kathleen Prager

grand-child

Chalice of pure joy!
Passed, like a sacrament
between devotees of a secret sect,
from youth to youth begetter,
the smile of understanding
the only password needed –
this child, dimpling and content
in the instinct knowledge of their adoration,
is the mirror image, and the vehicle
of the seed that passed and will pass
down countless generations.

Carol Evans

a prayer

When minds in the confusion of time
find words slur on the tongues helter-skelter,
and the thought's bright image
blurs under the burden of years,
when reason has dimmed the last lamp
and the candle flickers,
grant a swift slipping of the knot,
              no tears

Eunice Carter

index